Submitting Your Sponsorship Proposal Online

53 Companies that Accept Sponsorship Proposals Online - with Links

By Robert Villegas

Series Title: Finding Sponsors Volume 6

www.sponsorproaz.com

Introduction

If you are involved in sponsor search for your team, activity, or project, I'm sure you've come across those companies that require you to submit your proposal online by filling out a form that must be transmitted to them through the Internet. I wonder how many people just give up when they discover this or whether they investigate further and actually try to provide the needed information. Certainly, many of them learn that this is a tedious task because of the many questions you must answer.

Perhaps you wonder if this online submittal method is even worth the effort. Let's consider several facts about this process. Any company that would use an automated process for proposal submission has a problem with too many proposals coming in. They had too many proposals to review and the vast majority of them were of poor quality. This means that even if they were reading these proposals, they were not finding the information in them that enabled them to make a qualified decision about whether they wanted to pursue them. So, in order to create an evaluation process that was consistent with their marketing goals, they set up a system that would require the submitters of proposals to provide them with the information they needed so they could evaluate all proposals according to the same objective standards. They wanted to compare apples to apples, so to speak.

Automated submission accomplishes two goals for the sponsor. 1) if you don't have the information they need, you haven't thought through your value proposition, and you won't submit a good proposal. Most of them will reject proposals that aren't great looking. That's fine for them. They have saved a lot of money in not reviewing thousands of proposals. They just fill up their dumpsters with lots of paper. That means they don't have to waste valuable man hours reading proposals they don't want to see, and 2) when they get a proposal through the online submission process, they can evaluate it fairly against all the other proposals they receive, which means all submitted proposals receive a fair evaluation (you hope). To understand this issue, let's take a look at how companies evaluate proposals.

The process is called "valuation" and it is based upon a method that will enable the sponsor to determine how much money they will earn should they decide to sponsor you. A valuation takes the information you provide, meaning the information they require from you, and, based on their pre-programmed system, determines what their return on investment will be from your opportunity. Through this system, only the cream will rise to the top and, if you have a great opportunity, they will be calling you. This "valuation" enables the sponsor to fine tune its marketing program and devise ways to get more and more value for less and less money invested...which translates to a better bottom line.

So, the challenge for you is to send them the information they need and provide it to them through their online system. The good news is that most of the companies that require online submissions use the same company to help them value their proposals which means, in most cases, the information they require is similar. Sponsor Pro AZ has done a thorough review of many of these online submission systems, and we have come up with the most common questions they ask. You will find them below so you can prepare, in advance, the answers that will get you a fair hearing (Caveat: not every company asks the same questions so you should be prepared to carefully calculate every answer).

The good thing about this is that it can also provide you with an education. By looking at what these major sponsors require, you can also glean valuable information about your offering and ensure that the right information is provided by your other proposal submissions including in your sponsorship proposal for other companies that don't require online submission.

Finally, on the last pages of this document we've provided you with a list of the links to many companies that will accept online submissions.

Note: Sponsor Pro AZ provides no assurance that you will be sponsored by any of these companies. The features you provide may be the absolute best you can do (and be impressive) but you may still not be selected for an interview or meetings.

If you would like to work on these links on a desktop or laptop computer, go to www.sponsorproaz.com/input and you will find a page there with all the links.

Additionally, you can hire us to submit your proposal for you on line. The price for this service is $500.00. Give us a call and we can set it up for you.

Below are some of the common questions that marketers will want to see in your online submission.

Contact Information

First Name

Last Name

Job Title **Company or Organization Name**

Street Address **City**

State (U.S. only **Postal Code**

Country

Phone **Fax**

Email **Organization Website**

Are you a current customer?

Is your organization a non-profit?

Official Name of Opportunity or Event

Years in Existence for Event

Individual, Company or Organization Overseeing Opportunity

Opportunity Frequency

Geographic Range * - Indicate where your opportunity takes place (Select One –

Options include:

Markets - Specify the markets that your opportunity reaches.

Demographics – List the Demographics of your fans/spectators

Age

Income

Education

Rent/Own

Travel to events?

Race/Ethnic Group

Male Percentage

Female Percentage

Other

Locations/Dates

Locations/Dates

Sponsorship Packages and Benefits

Highlight the benefit(s) your opportunity offers to sponsors by clicking the appropriate checkboxes in the grid below. To submit your proposal, you must enter at least one sponsorship package.

List Amount needed for each sponsorship package:

List the marketing benefits of each sponsorship package:

Your best sales pitch in one paragraph – minimum of five sentences:

Please note: All listings in this document are *clickable*

Listings:

MassMutual Financial Group

https://www.massmutual.com/mmfg/pdf/corp_sponsorship.pdf

Wells Fargo

https://wellsfargosponsorships.com/home.aspx

US Bancorp

https://www.usbank.com/community/sponsorship/index.html

Sprint

https://sprint.versaic.com/login

Nike – product donations only

http://help-us.nikeinc.com/app/answers/detail/a_id/777/~/nike-sponsorship-and-donation-requests

Dr. Pepper/Snapple

https://drpeppersnapple.versaic.com/login

Nintendo

https://nintendo.versaic.com/login

Qatar Airways

http://www.qatarairways.com/za/en/sponsorship-application.page

Adobe

https://adobe.allegiancetech.com/cgi-bin/qwebcorporate.dll?idx=UK4FX6

Home Depot

https://hdepot.sponsor.com/

HSBC

https://hsbc.sponsor.com/

Publix Super Markets

http://corporate.publix.com/pages/sponsorship-request

Founders Brewing

http://foundersbrewing.hellosponsor.com/

Nikon USA

https://support.nikonusa.com/ci/documents/detail/5/95

Southern Tier Brewing Company

http://stbcbeer.hellosponsor.com/

RPM Outlet

https://www.rpmoutlet.com/sponsor.htm

Fidelity

https://www.fidelity.com/about-fidelity/corporate-sponsorship

DHL

http://www.dhl.com/en/about_us/partnerships/sponsorship_request.html

ginnybakes

http://ginnybakes.hellosponsor.com/

Target

https://corporate.target.com/about/sponsorship-request

Whole Me

http://wholeme.hellosponsor.com/

Coutts

https://coutts.sponsor.com/

Beanitos

http://beanitos.hellosponsor.com/

Lowes

https://lowes.versaic.com/login

Emirates

http://www.emirates.com/english/about/emirates-sponsorships/sponsorships.aspx

AleSmith Brewing

http://alesmith.hellosponsor.com/

JetBlue

https://jetblue.versaic.com/Login.aspx

Samsung

http://www.samsung.com/au/sponsorship/guidelines.html

Wegman's

https://wegmans.versaic.com/Login.aspx

Hershey's

https://hersheys.versaic.com/login

Giant Food

https://giantfood.versaic.com/login

Albertson's

https://albertsonscompaniesfoundation.versaic.com/login

Panera Bread

https://panerabread.versaic.com/login

Chiesi

https://chiesi.versaic.com/login

Brookshire's

https://brookshires.versaic.com/login

Fifth Third Bank
https://www.cybergrants.com/pls/cybergrants/quiz.display_question?x_gm_id=6990&x_quiz_id=9190

Highmark
https://www.highmark.com/about/corporate-responsibility/corporate-giving/grant-sponsorship-requests.html
Staples
https://staples.versaic.com/login

Denny's
https://dennys.versaic.com/login

Merck's (MSD)
https://msdcr.versaic.com/login

Marriott
https://marriott.versaic.com/login

CVS Health Gift Card
https://cvshealth.com/social-responsibility/our-giving/community-support

Alaska Air
https://alaskaair.versaic.com/login

Ozinga
https://ozingagiving.versaic.com/login

Wyndham
https://wyndham.versaic.com/login

Discover
https://discover.versaic.com/login

Stop&Shop
https://stopandshop.versaic.com/login/

Jack Links
https://jacklinks.versaic.com/login

Reliant
https://nrg.versaic.com/login

Citgo
https://citgo.versaic.com/login?returnurl=%2Fsubmitterproposalview%3Fdp%3DaWF0P

TlwMjEtMTAtMTggMTQ6NTE6MjJaJnBhcmFtcz1GRDpQcm9wb3NhbC5Qcm9wb3NhbElkWzMxMDVdJnNuPTQ5MWEzZDhmMDI3MTU1YmJhMzI3NWE0NTQyOGE3NDY3

Cracker Barrel
https://crackerbarrel.versaic.com/registration

ShopnSave
https://shopnsave.versaic.com/login

Coca-Cola
https://coca-colacompany.versaic.com/Simple/CocaColaCompany/TheCocaColaCompanyUnsolicitedSponsorshipProposalTypes1103092018.pdf

MUFG Union Bank Foundation
https://assets.unionbank.com/assets/file/about-us/mufg-union-bank-foundation-grant-guidelines-july-2020.pdf

Toyota

https://toyota--landing.sponsor.com/form?pid=0&cid=106628

RBC
https://rbc.sponsor.com/form?pid=0&cid=106648

Bombardier
https://bombardier.sponsor.com/form?pid=0&cid=106659

LL Bean
https://llbean.sponsor.com/form?pid=0&cid=106704

Santos
https://santos.sponsor.com/form

Herbalife
https://herbalife.sponsor.com/form?pid=0&cid=106743

About Robert Villegas

Robert Villegas is an Arizona resident who has spent his career working for several international transportation and technology companies. He is an Army veteran who served in Korea as a telecommunications specialist serving in the 7th Infantry Division in Camp Casey, Korea. He was educated in Indiana and earned a Degree through the University of the State of NY (Albany) via an external degree program. He is divorced with three grown children and three grandchildren.

About Sponsor Pro AZ (www.sponsorproaz.com)

Robert has also owned and managed a sport marketing firm named Insight Marketing Group and several subsidiaries one of which is known as Sponsor Pro AZ which specializes in sponsor search, sponsorship and grant proposal creations, Business Plans, websites, proposal briefs, branding documents, websites and more.

From our headquarters in Phoenix, AZ, (originally Indianapolis, IN) we have created documents for business startups, athletes, professional and amateur sports teams, entertainment professionals, concert promoters and sponsors from all over the world. Our document prices will help you make efficient use of your marketing dollars.

Business Plans and Sponsorship Proposals make up the bulk of our work. We have created hundreds of such documents to help our clients in their vital fundraising efforts. We are producing some of the best sponsorship proposals and business plans today.

Sponsor Pro AZ Sponsorship Proposal Service Packages for Sports Teams, Athletes and Entertainment Event Promoters

Your sponsorship proposal is your most important business document. It must be professionally done and clearly promote the value you bring to your potential sponsor's marketing plan. Your proposal must be attractive and to the point.

We can create your sponsorship proposal as a single item or as part of a Customized Service Package. Go to our website at https://www.sponsorproaz.com/#SPONSORSHIPPROPOSALS then call us to place your order: 1-317-881-3826.

Sponsor Pro AZ is also producing the following types of documents:

Business Cards and Stationery

T-shirt Design

Smart gal
PRODUCTIONS

Logos

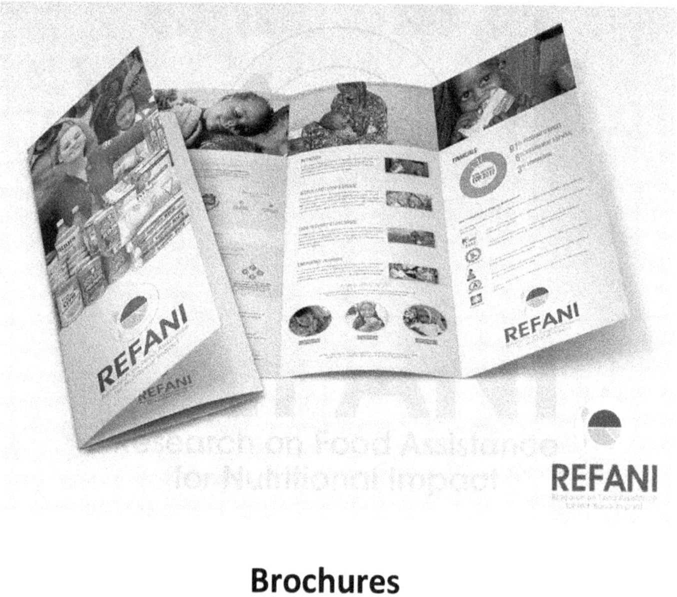

Brochures

HOSTED BY:
Miami-Dade County Commissioner Audrey M. Edmonson
and The Black Archives Historic Lyric Theater
PRESENTED BY:
Latonja Eppinger, SMART GAL Productions and Suzanne Boyd, THE PARTY COMPANY
THE FILM
BLACK FRIDAY
What Legacy Will You Leave?
when you die will you leave bills or benefits?
Sponsored By:
OneUnited
BANK
The film champions financial literacy and the importance of leaving a secure future for the next generation.
To RSVP for the screening, email Sboydparty@aol.com.
For VIP Package information, call 800-385-1819.
Miami's Premiere Movie Screening
Panel Discussion Immediately Following
Friday, February 12, 2016
Doors open at 7 pm
Film Promptly at 8 pm
The Historic Lyric Theater
819 NW 2nd Ave
Miami, FL 33136
"Dessert Reception To End The Night Sweetly"

Flyers

ABOUT ME

Business Books by Robert Villegas

These four books by Robert Villegas comprise some of the business books that he has written. As an executive working for several companies, he was able to develop these methods that will help anyone seeking to excel in the business world. These books are:

How to Be a Great Employee – and a Greater Manager

You cannot be a great manager without first being a great employee. And this is something that requires learning, experience and attitude. The attitude comes from you but the learning and experience you should acquire through diligent study and practice. http://amzn.to/2BqdG2i $3.99 Kindle $8.95 softcover

SWOT Analysis Supercharged

A SWOT Analysis is an objective look at the internal and external elements of your organization that impact your success or lack thereof. If done diligently, you will always have a handle on what you need to do to improve season after season. http://amzn.to/2BCAWYx $3.99 Kindle $6.95 softcover

The Five-Module Call Center Training System

The Five-Module Call Center Training System is designed to assist the Call Center Team Leader in helping his employees quickly upgrade their skills to an acceptable level. http://amzn.to/2B3Svj1 $3.99 Kindle $5.95 softcover

Website Development Methodology

Effective strategic marketing requires the ability to differentiate the website development organization and its deliverables from those of the competition. http://amzn.to/2DnYMqh $2.99 Kindle $12.95 softcover.

www.robertvillegas.com

Books on Sport and Entertainment Sponsorship

Finding Sponsors 1 and 2

This book is written for anyone seeking sponsorship relationships in the sport and entertainment fields. The ideas and principles presented here are applicable to any company, sport team, entertainment company, marketing agency and charitable organization that uses corporate sponsorships to support its activities. Volume 1: https://amzn.to/3ejm1Hp $5.19 Kindle $12.95 softcover Volume 2: https://amzn.to/3eVDo0e $4.69 Kindle $10.95 softcover

How to Write a Sponsorship Proposal

This booklet provide you with some basic guidelines on what to communicate in order to produce a winning sponsorship proposal. These guidelines will focus on what you should be presenting to your potential sponsor to make the best business case for involvement with your team or entertainment company. $2.99 Kindle $6.95 softcover

Hospitality Event Planning Handbook

One key part of your sponsorship activation strategy might be customer hospitality events in conjunction with sporting events. How do you pull off a Hospitality Event for your biggest customers? You may not know how to start, what to do and how to ensure the event is a success. This book can help. http://amzn.to/2mxzpgy $7.95 softcover.

Selling Sponsorship in the Age of the Coronavirus

This book provides suggestions on how sport teams, athletes and concert promoters can mitigate the damage done to their businesses by the economic lockdowns (due to the Coronavirus). It integrates checklists, SWOT Analysis and other valuable business aids into one toolkit that will help you keep your sport and/or genre alive in these difficult times. https://amzn.to/2QVBNiM $5.15 Kindle $5.95 softcover

www.robertvillegas.com

Books on Sponsorship and Business

Finding Sponsors Forms Book

This "Forms Book" is intended to provide samples of the forms mentioned in my book "Finding Sponsors for Sport and Entertainment". This will make it possible for you to reproduce these forms in other formats as well as download the forms document from the SponsorProAZ website for use with Microsoft Word. https://amzn.to/3b95yDW $2.99 Kindle $5.50 softcover

Submitting Your Sponsorship Proposal Online

This booklet enables sport teams and concert promoters to submit their sponsorship proposals to companies that accept only online submission of proposals. https://amzn.to/3euzdti $2.99 Kindle $5.95 softcover

The Art of Sponsorship

This short book is based upon Mr. Villegas' book "Finding Sponsors for Sport and Entertainment". It is also based upon a course that he taught for an organization managing Indiana Parks and Recreation facilities. It is, in a sense, a condensation of information from the book geared toward organizations that would like to earn revenues on their facilities through corporate sponsorship. https://amzn.to/3beuVnC $2.99 Kinde $6.95 softcover.

Restarting Your Business After the Pandemic

This new book is designed to help you restart your business after the Coronavirus pandemic. You will find here all the right questions, how you can find the answers and the forms you need to walk through your restart and coming success. https://amzn.to/2QVBNiM $5.15 Kindle $5.95 softcover

www.robertvillegas.com

www.ingramcontent.com/pod-product-compliance
Lightning Source LLC
Chambersburg PA
CBHW070341190526
45169CB00005B/1990
9781537596167